Talking

T

T

Jilly Attwood

www.heinemann.co.uk/library
Visit our website to find out more information about **Heinemann Library** books.

To order:
☎ Phone 44 (0) 1865 888066
▤ Send a fax to 44 (0) 1865 314091
▣ Visit the Heinemann Bookshop at www.heinemann.co.uk/library to browse our catalogue and order online.

First published in Great Britain by Heinemann Library, Halley Court, Jordan Hill, Oxford OX2 8EJ, part of Harcourt Education.
Heinemann is a registered trademark of Harcourt Education Ltd.

Editorial: Kathy Peltan and Kate Bellamy
Design: Jo Hinton-Malivoire and bigtop, Bicester, UK
Picture Research: Ruth Blair
Production: Séverine Ribierre

Originated by Dot Gradations Ltd
Printed and bound in China by South China Printing Company

ISBN 0 431 07941 2 (hardback)
09 08 07 06 05
10 9 8 7 6 5 4 3 2 1

ISBN 0 431 07946 3 (paperback)
09 08 07 06 05
10 9 8 7 6 5 4 3 2 1

British Library Cataloguing in Publication Data
Attwood, Jilly
529.7
Talking about time: Times of the day
A full catalogue record for this book is available from the British Library.

Acknowledgements
The publishers would like to thank the following for permission to reproduce photographs: Corbis p. **13**; Corbis/RF p. **5**; Getty Images/Photodisc pp. **14**, **16**; Harcourt Education pp. **4**, **9**, **18a**, **18b** (Tudor Photography), **6**, **15**, **17** (Trevor Clifford), **7**, **10**, **12**, **19**, **20**, **21** (Gareth Boden), **11** (Martin Sookias), **15** (Anthony King); John Walmsley p. **8**.

Cover photograph of boy asleep in bed, reproduced with permission of Harcourt Education (Gareth Boden).

Our thanks to Annie Davy for her assistance in the preparation of this book.

Every effort has been made to contact copyright holders of any material reproduced in this book. Any omissions will be rectified in subsequent printings if notice is given to the publishers.

The paper used to print this book comes from sustainable resources.

2

Contents

It's morning!

Rise and shine!

4

It's time to get up.
It's time to get dressed.

It's time for breakfast

What do you like to eat for breakfast?

Brush, brush, brush!

It's time to clean your teeth.

It's time to go

It's time to go to school.

How do you get to school?

It's time to go to work too.

It's school time

It's time to paint. Do you like painting?

Splat

It's story time!

What is your favourite story?

It's lunch time

It's time for lunch.

Yummy! Yummy!

12

After lunch it's playtime.

Hooray!

After school time

What do you like to do after school?

It's dinner time

It's time to get dinner ready.

Do you help to make dinner?

What's your favourite dinner?

It's fun time

What do you do after dinner?

It's bed time

It's time to get ready for bed.

It's time to clean your teeth again.

Time for sleep.
Night night!

What's the time?

Index

Notes for adults

The *Talking about time* series introduces young children to the concept of time. By relating their own experiences to specific moments in time, the children can start to explore the pattern of regular events that occur in a day, week or year. The following Early Learning Goals are relevant to this series:

Knowledge and understanding of the world
Early learning goals for a sense of time
• find out about past and present events in their own lives, and in those of their families and other people they know
Early learning goals for exploration and investigation
• find out about, and identify, some features of events they observe
• look closely at similarities, differences, patterns and change
Early learning goals for cultures and beliefs
• describe significant events for family or friends

This book shows the significant events that take place in most children's lives over the course of a day. The events are given in chronological order to aid children's thought about the passing of time during the day. The book encourages children to discuss why something happens at a particular time of day. Simple clock times introduce children to the conventional way of showing time.

Follow-up activities
• Draw the events that your child experiences during a day of the week on separate pieces of card. Mix up the cards and ask the child to place them in the correct time sequence, while discussing what happens before and after each event.
• Throughout the day, incidentally point out hour times on a clock and link them with important landmarks that occur in the morning, afternoon and at night.